For Rory and Hana,
with love forever
– Rachel Greener

For Lauri, who is like
a sister to me
– Sandra de la Prada

First published 2026 by Nosy Crow Ltd
Wheat Wharf, 27a Shad Thames
London, SE1 2XZ, UK

Nosy Crow Eireann Ltd
44 Orchard Grove, Kenmare,
Co Kerry, V93 FY22, Ireland

www.nosycrow.com

ISBN 978 1 80513 975 1 (HB)
ISBN 978 1 80513 976 8 (PB)

Text by Rachel Greener

A CIP catalogue record for this book is available from the British Library.

Printed in China following rigorous ethical sourcing standards.

1 3 5 7 9 8 6 4 2 (HB)
1 3 5 7 9 8 6 4 2 (PB)

Our New Baby

Written by
Rachel Greener

Illustrated by
Sandra de la Prada

nosy crow

Do you know where you lived,
before you lived here?

You grew in a tummy,
for weeks

This is you
when you were in
Mama's tummy!

and weeks

and weeks.

And then,
one day . . .

you were born!

You met your family,

and they took
you home.

When you were hungry,
your family gave you milk.

When you couldn't sleep, your family cuddled you.

And when you did a wee or a poo . . .

your family changed your nappies.

But now,
a new baby
has come home.

And you are
the big kid.

Even though you are
still *quite* small.

When the new baby is hungry,
they will need feeding.

And you might
have to wait
a little bit longer
for your food.

When you can't sleep . . .

. . . it might be because
the new baby can't sleep.

And when you need
a wee . . .

. . . you might have to wait
a bit longer than you would like,
to get the help you need.

The grown-ups in your family
might be very tired for a while.

You might find you are spending more time
playing with your aunties or your uncles,
or your granny or grandpa . . .

. . . or at nursery or school.

And that can be fun!

Sometimes it might seem
that the new baby gets
so many cuddles . . .

. . . and so many smiles,
and so many snuggles.

You might even want
to be a baby again.

And sometimes, for a moment . . .
your family might almost forget
that you are still *quite* small.

But even though sharing
can be hard . . .

having someone to share
things with can be very special.

Because now,
there is someone
new to love you.

To watch you.
To listen to you.
To smile at you.
To look up to you.

And there is someone new
for you to love in return.

And although you will have
to wait a little while . . .

babies don't stay
babies forever.

They grow up into brilliant
big kids. Just like you.